Better Way
30 Day Daily Devotional

Your Best Day Today

Rev. Ron Walker

Copyright©2010, 2016
Better Way Ministries, Inc. and
Ron Walker

All rights reserved. No part of this publication may be reproduced or transmitted for commercial purposes, except for brief quotations, without written permission of the publisher.

Churches and other noncommercial interests may reproduce portions of this book without the express written permission of Better Way Ministries, Inc. providing that the text does not exceed approximately 500 words. When reproducing text from this book, include the following credit line: "From Your Best Day Today, published by Better Way Ministries and Rev. Ron Walker. Used by permission."

ISBN-13: 978-1539782230
ISBN-10: 1539782239

All scriptures unless otherwise noted are taken from the New International Version of the Bible.

Published by Better Way Ministries, Inc. PO Box 223, Lovejoy, Georgia 30228. BetterWay2009@gmail.com.

Our mission is to demonstrate that "There is a Better Way to Live, Love and Do Business."

Contents

1. Just Do It
2. Fear Nothing
3. Abstain from Sin
4. Praise God
5. I Am Better
6. Be Content
7. Have Fun
8. Choose to Be Happy
9. Rejoice No Matter What
10. Watch Your Mouth
11. I Am Somebody
12. Get More Passionate
13. Produce Fruit
14. Produce More Fruit
15. Look with the Eyes of the Prophet
16. Don't Stop Running
17. Hear the Call
18. Go and Be Great
19. Soar like The Eagles
20. Display His Splendor
21. Get Up
22. Think Happy Thoughts
23. Remember What God Has Done
24. Cleanse Your Heart
25. Forgive
26. Never Give Up
27. Focus On the Right Stuff
28. Inherit What God Promised You
29. Hear the Abundance
30. Sow a Seed

Day 1: **Just Do It**
(John 2:1-10)

¹ On the third day a wedding took place at Cana in Galilee. Jesus' mother was there,
² and Jesus and his disciples had also been invited to the wedding.
³ When the wine was gone, Jesus' mother said to him, "They have no more wine."
⁴ "Woman, why do you involve me?" Jesus replied. "My hour has not yet come."
⁵ His mother said to the servants, "Do whatever he tells you."
⁶ Nearby stood six stone water jars, the kind used by the Jews for ceremonial washing, each holding from twenty to thirty gallons.
⁷ Jesus said to the servants, "Fill the jars with water"; so they filled them to the brim.
⁸ Then he told them, "Now draw some out and take it to the master of the banquet." They did so,
⁹ and the master of the banquet tasted the water that had been turned into wine. He did not realize where it had come from, though the servants who had drawn the water knew. Then he called the bridegroom aside
¹⁰ and said, "Everyone brings out the choice wine first and then the cheaper wine after the guests have had too much to drink; but you have saved the best till now."

Day 1: **Just Do It!**

The time has come to move past the excuses and move into your destiny. WHATEVER He says do, just do it! Jesus is not one for excuses or doubts. He tells his mother that His time has not yet come, but He still does the miraculous.

God is not concerned with our weaknesses, our pasts, our flaws or our excuses. He just wants us to do what He asks so that He can make miracles happen. When we become more obedient to the Word and Will of God it allows the Lord to move in a mighty way. It's our disobedience and doubt that keeps the Lord from doing the great things that He wants to do. Don't let this be another day that you stop God from doing great things in your life. Open up and look for God to move in your life today.

Be ye holy, be ye just, be kind and be loving, don't fret and do not doubt. Whatever He says do, Just Do It!

The Word of God tells us to work as unto the Lord, do it. The Word tells us not to be lazy, well. It tells us to act in excellence, this is practical. If you put these things into action you are bound to succeed. You don't have to look for the Heavens to open and have a dark cloud speak to you to know what God is saying do. It's right in His word. Just Do It!

Daily Declaration

Today will be the best day of my life. I will not let anything or anyone stop me from reaching my potential. I am the righteousness of God and I will do whatever God says do. Today will be the best day of my life because I will Just Do It in Jesus' name.

Day 2: **Fear Nothing**
(Jeremiah 1:1-8)

¹ The words of Jeremiah the son of Hilkiah, of the priests who were in Anathoth in the land of Benjamin, ² to whom the word of the Lord came in the days of Josiah the son of Amon, king of Judah, in the thirteenth year of his reign.

³ It came also in the days of Jehoiakim the son of Josiah, king of Judah, until the end of the eleventh year of Zedekiah the son of Josiah, king of Judah, until the carrying away of Jerusalem captive in the fifth month.

⁴ Then the word of the Lord came to me, saying:

⁵ "Before I formed you in the womb I knew you; Before you were born I sanctified you; I ordained you a prophet to the nations."

⁶ Then said I: "Ah, Lord God! Behold, I cannot speak, for I am a youth."

⁷ But the Lord said to me: "Do not say, I am a youth, for you shall go to all to whom I send you, and whatever I command you, you shall speak.

⁸ Do not be afraid of their faces, for I am with you to deliver you," says the Lord.

Day 2: **Fear Nothing**

You were called to this so fear nothing. People often tell me that they are unsure of their purpose or their calling, but then won't stop talking about certain goals, dreams or visions they have. Whatever is burning in your heart, clanging in your mind and chasing you constantly has been put there by God. He called you to do that thing that is in you. Whatever it is that you really want to do and just can't seem to shake or out run could very well be your destiny. Stop running, stop making excuses, stop trying to figure out why you can't do it, and most importantly, stop being afraid, Fear Nothing.

God has called you into greatness. He has ordained you for this, appointed you to this and created you just to do this! Before you were formed, before you were born, God knew you and He knew what He wanted you to do. He appointed Jeremiah as a prophet to the nations and he appointed you as something as well. He declares in verse 8 that He is with you and will rescue you. Why, because He wants you to fulfill your purpose. Fear Nothing!

The Lord is watching over you. Focus on your destiny, not on your troubles or your enemies or your phobias or your fears. Focus on your purpose. If you don't know it yet, then focus on praising and worshipping God because if nothing else, you were created to worship Christ!

I believe in you, God believes in you, so fear nothing and focus on being the person that God created you to be. Fear Nothing!

Daily Declaration

Today will be the best day of my life. I was created for a reason and I have a purpose to fulfill. Therefore, I will focus on the Lord and not on fear. Today will be the best day of my life because I will Fear Nothing in Jesus' name.

Day 3: **Abstain from Sin**
(Isaiah 59:1-8)

¹ Behold, the Lord's hand is not shortened, that it cannot save; nor His ear heavy, that it cannot hear.

² But your iniquities have separated you from your God; and your sins have hidden His face from you, so that He will not hear.

³ For your hands are defiled with blood, and your fingers with iniquity; your lips have spoken lies, your tongue has muttered perversity.

⁴ No one calls for justice, nor does any plead for truth. They trust in empty words and speak lies; they conceive evil and bring forth iniquity.

⁵They hatch vipers' eggs and weave the spider's web; he who eats of their eggs dies, and from that which is crushed a viper breaks out.

⁶ Their webs will not become garments, nor will they cover themselves with their works; their works are works of iniquity, and the act of violence is in their hands.

⁷Their feet run to evil and they make haste to shed innocent blood; their thoughts are thoughts of iniquity, wasting and destruction are in their paths. ⁸The way of peace they have not known and there is no justice in their ways; they have made themselves crooked paths; whoever takes that way shall not know peace.

Day 3: **Abstain from Sin**

Sin separates us from God, but we should be motivated by the fact that Jesus died for the remission of our sins. Sin is not okay. Sin separates us and kills our motivation and momentum. Don't let sin steal your peace, joy and motivation or momentum today. You have been created for greatness, and no sin can keep you from that greatness unless you allow it to. Abstain from sin this day and make today the best day of your life.

Sin acts as a cancer when you are saved. It causes you to become sluggish and incapable of performing at optimum godly levels. Sin robs the mind, body and soul of things that are important to leading a prosperous life, such as peace. Refuse to let sin rob you anymore. Don't focus on never sinning again, just focus on not sinning today! Don't set the bar so high that you don't even try to reach it. Set the bar high enough to challenge you, but low enough to reach it.

No matter how much you have sinned or what sin you have committed, God's arm is not too short to save you. Be motivated and encouraged today because you realize that God can still save you from whatever is going on in your life. Simply focus this day on abstaining from sin.

Daily Declaration

Today will be the best day of my life. I will abstain from sin and I will not allow sin to steal my peace or rob me of my joy. Guilt will not stop me. Sin will not stop me. Nothing will stop me. Today will be the best day of my life because I will Abstain From Sin in Jesus' name.

Day 4: **Praise God**
(Psalms 150)

[1] Praise the Lord!
Praise God in His sanctuary;
Praise Him in His mighty firmament!

[2] Praise Him for His mighty acts;
Praise Him according to His excellent greatness!

[3] Praise Him with the sound of the trumpet;
Praise Him with the lute and harp!

[4] Praise Him with the timbrel and dance;
Praise Him with stringed instruments and flutes!

[5] Praise Him with loud cymbals;
Praise Him with clashing cymbals!

[6] Let everything that has breath praise the Lord.
Praise the Lord!

Day 4: Praise God

You might not have everything that you want, but I am sure that you have something to praise God for. Let this day be full of praise. Look for new ways to praise God. Find a way to praise Him in everything that you do. God is worthy of being praised. He birthed you, he built you and He blessed you to be great and to meet the challenges of this day. No matter what you come into contact with today, remember to praise God.

God is the ultimate motivator and the best encourager available and all that He asks us to do is praise Him. He's the biggest giver and the best friend we could ever have. He owns the cattle of a thousand hills. He formed the Earth and all them that dwell in it. He is God your strength and your joy, your rock and your salvation, your fortress and strong tower. God is your savior. Without Him we are nothing, but because of Him we can have everything. He deserves our praise.

Praising God in itself can serve as a motivator. When we truly praise God, the negatives of life must fade away and our joy should be enhanced. The Bible says that if we lift God up (praise Him) that He will draw us nearer to Him meaning that He will raise us up. He will not allow us to remain in the muck and miry clay of life. He will allow us to pass over it so praise God this day because He deserves it and we need it. Let everything that has breath praise the Lord. I hope that includes you.

Daily Declaration

Today will be the best day of my life. I will praise God and I will not let anything stifle my praise. I will praise Him wherever I go and in all that I do. Today will be the best day of my life because I will Praise God in Jesus' name.

Day 5: **I Am Better**
(1 Corinthians 13:8-12)

[8] Love never fails. But whether there are prophecies, they will fail; whether there are tongues, they will cease; whether there is knowledge, it will vanish away.

[9] For we know in part and we prophesy in part.

[10] But when that which is perfect has come, then that which is in part will be done away.

[11] When I was a child, I spoke as a child, I understood as a child, I thought as a child; but when I became a man, I put away childish things.

[12] For now we see in a mirror, dimly, but then face to face. Now I know in part, but then I shall know just as I also am known.

Day 5: **I Am Better**

You might not be where you want to be, but thank God that you're not where you used to be. You might not be the man or woman that you hoped you would be by now, but thank God that you are better. I'm sure that you can look back over your life and see that you've grown some. I'm sure that if you do a self-analysis and check who you were five, ten, or one year ago, you will see some change. You might not be who you want to be, but let's be thankful today that we're better.

Give God glory today because He saw you through last year, provided for you last month and gave you life today. I know that you have something to be thankful for today, so put all of the stuff that happened yesterday out of your mind. Forget about your past and what you thought your future would look like. Take the time to thank God for today. You may have thought that you would be further by now, but God knew where you would be and in spite of that He decided to love you anyhow.

The Bible tells us that Jesus is perfect and that we should aspire to be like Him, but the truth of the matter is that sometimes we mess up, sometimes we fail, sometimes we complain and sometimes we become nostalgic and think that we were better off in yesteryear, but truthfully YOU ARE BETTER NOW, than you were before. Thank God that you are better. You might not be the best. You might not be perfect. You might not be all that you wanted to be, but thank God today that you are better!

Daily Declaration

Today will be the best day of my life. I will not stress over where I am. I will not fret over where I thought I would be. I will focus on thanking God that I am better than I used to be. Today will be the best day of my life because I will Thank God because I Am Better in Jesus' name.

Day 6: **Be Content**
(Hebrews 13:5)

[5] Let your conduct be without covetousness; be content with such things as you have. For He Himself has said, "I will never leave you nor forsake you."

Day 6: **Be Content**

That scripture is big enough all by itself. Try focusing on that alone for the day and remember it. Don't let money control your life. Don't become so focused on the acquisition of assets that you become discontented with your life. You were put on this earth for a much greater reason than to just get rich. Riches and the love money can separate us from our ultimate purpose. Money in its self is neither good nor bad, it is our motivation behind getting it and what we do with it that becomes good or bad.

There is a story of a rich man that came to Jesus and asked Jesus about receiving eternal life. Jesus told him to sell all that he had and give it to the poor. The man walked away very sad because he could not deal with the thought of parting with his money. Money should not have such as hold on us that it keeps us from honoring God and fulfilling our true purpose in life. Spend this day trying to become more content with your life and what you have. Be content with your talent, your family, your job, your home, your car, your joy, your peace, your body, your mind, your intellect, your education, your church, your pastor, your God!

I know it's not the popular thing to say and it's not what most people want to here, but just be happy with what you have. It's not a bad thing if you strive for more. I implore you to go for the gold, but be content if you end up with the silver. It's not the end of the world if you don't have everything that you want. Be happy that you have as much as you do because need I say, you could have a lot less. Be content.

Daily Declaration

Today will be the best day of my life. I will be content in all things because God has been good to me and I am thankful for all that I have. I will strive for more, but be happy with what I have. Today will be the best day of my life because I will Be Content in Jesus' name.

Day 7: **Have Fun**
(Ecclesiastes 3:1-4)

[1] To everything there is a season,
A time for every purpose under heaven:

[2] A time to be born,
And a time to die;
A time to plant,
And a time to pluck what is planted;

[3] A time to kill,
And a time to heal;
A time to break down,
And a time to build up;

[4] A time to weep,
And a time to laugh;
A time to mourn,
And a time to dance;

Day 7: **Have Fun**

Some people walk through life with a permanent snarl on their face. They seem unpleasant, unhappy and unapproachable and these are Christians. Why would anyone want to be a part of something that seems so sad? Have Fun. Just relax. Christ died so that we could have an abundant life. A part of the abundance is joy. Some have ventured to believe that the joy of the Lord is their salvation. I'm one of them.

Joy can save you from a bad day. Joy can lift you out of a bad situation. Joy can help you keep your Christianity when people try to make you lose your religion, so to speak. So just have fun. Don't take everything so seriously. Spend this day focusing on keeping a smile on your face, joy in your heart and just have fun!

That means if someone cuts you off on your way to work, just smile. If someone steps on your foot, insults your new look, calls you out your name, and talks about your mother, you let them know that this is still the best day of your life and that God is still in control. Just take a breath, relax, laugh and be joyful. This is still the day that the Lord has made. He woke you up this morning because He has a purpose for you so don't let anyone deny you of your purposeful day by stealing your joy. Sometimes we don't realize it, but today's purpose could be to simply have fun and show someone else that it is possible to smile even when everything is not perfect.

There is a time for everything and now is the time to be joyful and Have Fun. Rejoice this day because the Lord is good and he saw fit to give you one more day. Hallelujah!

Daily Declaration

Today will be the best day of my life. I will have fun and enjoy my life this day. I will not allow anyone or anything to steal my joy. Today will be the best day of my life because I will Have Fun in Jesus' name.

Day 8: **Choose to Be Happy**
(Isaiah 61:1-3)

[1] "The Spirit of the Lord God is upon Me, because the Lord has anointed Me to preach good tidings to the poor; He has sent Me to heal the brokenhearted, to proclaim liberty to the captives, and the opening of the prison to those who are bound;

[2] To proclaim the acceptable year of the Lord, and the day of vengeance of our God; to comfort all who mourn,

[3] To console those who mourn in Zion, to give them beauty for ashes, the oil of joy for mourning, the garment of praise for the spirit of heaviness; that they may be called trees of righteousness, the planting of the Lord, that He may be glorified."

Day 8: **Choose to Be Happy**

Do you realize that you choose whether or not to be happy? It's true. We decide to either be happy or sad. The Word of God says that I will give you beauty for ashes, and praise for depression. It is our decision whether to keep the spirit of depression or take the garment of praise.

I want you to truly examine yourself and your life today and find ways to be happy or happier. God put you here as a demonstration of what He can do. He wants to display His splendor, His grace, and His majesty through your happiness. Believe it or not, God finds joy in your happiness so let's make God happy today by choosing to be happy.

The statements made by Isaiah in chapter 61 are a part of Messianic prophecy. We see that in Luke 4 Jesus applies these statements to Himself. He later tells us that we would do greater works. So with all this said, you don't have time to be down! You have work to do. There are poor people that need to hear the Gospel, bound people that need to be loosed and blind people that are waiting to recover their sight. It's our job to declare freedom to the captives and proclaim this to be the acceptable year of the Lord and we can do all this by demonstrating our joy, exuding happiness and being a blessing to the people we come into contact with on a daily basis.

God has blessed you. Perhaps not in every way you want to be, but in some way. I am sure that you can find something to be happy about this day. Choose to be happy. Choose the garment of praise. Choose to make this the best day of your life. It's all up to you.

Daily Declaration

Today will be the best day of my life. I will choose to be happy and I will not allow sadness or depression to creep in and rule my life. Today will be the best day of my life because I will Choose to Be Happy in Jesus' name.

Day 9: **Rejoice No Matter What (James 1:2-4)**

² My brethren, count it all joy when you fall into various trials,

³ knowing that the testing of your faith produces patience.

⁴ But let patience have its perfect work, that you may be perfect and complete, lacking nothing.

Day 9: **Rejoice No Matter What**

God wants us to be complete. That is true prosperity. He does not just want you to have money and material things. He wants you to have joy, peace, patience and wisdom. He wants you to rejoice always because everything that happens in your life is adding to who God wants you to be. The good things that happen, add. The bad things that happen, add. Everything that happens adds to your life and ultimately completes you and makes you a better person.

Spend this day looking at everything that happens to you as a blessing because it is. Rejoice when seemingly bad things happen because they are adding to your wholeness this day. Rejoice because God is working overtime to develop your faith and perseverance and push you closer to your purpose. Focus today on rejoicing.

If you are still alive, there is still room for you to grow. You might be living in your purpose right now, but there is always room for growth. Everything that happens to you is to help you grow and mature. All Christians must continue to mature as we walk down this path of righteousness. Until we get to Heaven and see Jesus, there will be some things that we will have to deal with, but through it all we must rejoice.

Daily Declaration

Today will be the best day of my life. Today I will rejoice because everything that happens to me will work out for my good. I will not worry. I will only rejoice. Today will be the best day of my life because I will Rejoice No Matter What in Jesus' name.

Day 10: **Watch Your Mouth**
(James 3:6-12)

⁶ And the tongue is a fire, a world of iniquity. The tongue is so set among our members that it defiles the whole body, and sets on fire the course of nature; and it is set on fire by hell.

⁷ For every kind of beast and bird, of reptile and creature of the sea, is tamed and has been tamed by mankind.

⁸ But no man can tame the tongue. It is an unruly evil, full of deadly poison.

⁹ With it we bless our God and Father, and with it we curse men, who have been made in the similitude of God.

¹⁰ Out of the same mouth proceed blessing and cursing. My brethren, these things ought not to be so.

¹¹ Does a spring send forth fresh water and bitter from the same opening?

¹² Can a fig tree, my brethren, bear olives, or a grapevine bear figs? Thus no spring yields both salt water and fresh.

Day 10: **Watch Your Mouth**

How many times have we seen people praising on Sunday and cussing on Monday, worshipping at Wednesday night bible study and lying at work on Thursday? There are too many Christians living double lives with their tongue. The tongue is a tool and as with any tool it does what the master of the tool tells it to do. Your tongue can conjure up lies or produce blessings. It can tear down people or lift up nations. It is all our choice.

The Word of God in verse 10 says that this should not be. We all know it happens, but it shouldn't. It is time to hold people accountable for the actions of their tongues, but let's focus on our own first. Spend this day watching your mouth. Let's get the plank out of our eye before trying to remove a splinter from another person's eye. Watch your mouth and see if you are one of those people pulling double duty with your tongue.

Don't use your tongue for yelling, cussing and lying. Use it for blessing, uplifting and praising. This is the day that the Lord has made, let's be glad and rejoice in it. He gave you that tongue to praise and lift Him up so that He can draw you closer to Him. God wants to be close to you, but when you let your tongue spew out venom and produce sour speech, God withdraws.

If you want a closer walk with God, watch your mouth. Let's make this the best day of our lives by watching our mouths. Be careful not to insult people, hurt people or curse people with your tongue. Be who God created you to be, a worshipper. Use your tongue to praise God and be sure to watch your mouth.

Daily Declaration

Today will be the best day of my life. Today I will make sure to watch my mouth. I will not use my tongue for evil, but for good. I will uplift and not tear down. Today will be the best day of my life because I will Watch My Mouth in Jesus' name.

Day 11: **I Am Somebody**
(1 Peter 2:4-10)

[4] Coming to Him as to a living stone, rejected indeed by men, but chosen by God and precious,

[5] you also, as living stones, are being built up a spiritual house, a holy priesthood, to offer up spiritual sacrifices acceptable to God through Jesus Christ.

[6] Therefore it is also contained in the Scripture, "Behold, I lay in Zion a chief cornerstone, elect, precious, and he who believes on Him will by no means be put to shame."

[7] Therefore, to you who believe, He is precious; but to those who are disobedient, "The stone which the builders rejected has become the chief cornerstone," [8] and "A stone of stumbling and a rock of offense." They stumble, being disobedient to the word, to which they also were appointed.

[9] But you are a chosen generation, a royal priesthood, a holy nation, His own special people, that you may proclaim the praises of Him who called you out of darkness into His marvelous light; [10] who once were not a people but are now the people of God, who had not obtained mercy but now have obtained mercy.

Day 11: **I Am Somebody**

If you didn't believe that you were something, you should now. The Word of God says that you are a chosen people, a royal priesthood and a holy nation. You are somebody. The Bible says that you belong to God! My God, you are somebody! That should be enough to get you excited. Today is going to be the best day of your life because you belong to God. God has laid claim on you and all you have to do is accept Him. How could you ask for a better deal?

Those that reject Him will stumble and fall, but not you. You have something to stand on, the cornerstone! He will not allow you to be put to shame. He will comfort you, care for you and bless you. You are His people and possess His mercy. Your life is getting ready to turn around and get even better because you are starting to realize the power that you possess. There is greatness in you and God put it there because you are a part of His people.

God is lifting you up to show the nation how to be holy. He is setting you apart because you have been chosen. This word is yours and the power of God belongs to you. It is not by coincidence that you are reading these words. God made it possible. Spend this day rejoicing because you are a chosen people, a royal priesthood and a holy nation. You belong to God and yes you are special. You are somebody!

Daily Declaration

Today will be the best day of my life. Today I declare that I am somebody. I am God's people. I belong to the Lord Most High and I have been chosen by Him. Today will be the best day of my life because I Am Somebody in Jesus' name.

Day 12: **Get More Passionate**
(1 Samuel 17:34-40)

[34] But David said to Saul, "Your servant has been keeping his father's sheep. When a lion or a bear came and carried off a sheep from the flock,

[35] I went after it, struck it and rescued the sheep from its mouth. When it turned on me, I seized it by its hair, struck it and killed it.

[36] Your servant has killed both the lion and the bear; this uncircumcised Philistine will be like one of them, because he has defied the armies of the living God.

[37] The LORD who delivered me from the paw of the lion and the paw of the bear will deliver me from the hand of this Philistine." Saul said to David, "Go, and the LORD be with you."

[38] Then Saul dressed David in his own tunic. He put a coat of armor on him and a bronze helmet on his head.

[39] David fastened on his sword over the tunic and tried walking around, because he was not used to them. "I cannot go in these," he said to Saul, "because I am not used to them." So he took them off.

[40] Then he took his staff in his hand, chose five smooth stones from the stream, put them in the pouch of his shepherd's bag and, with his sling in his hand, approached the Philistine.

Day 12: **Get More Passionate**

We overcome by the blood of the Lamb and the word of our testimony. Do you realize that David overcame the giant simply based on his testimony? He said that God saved me from the lion and he saved me from the bear, what reason would I have to believe that He can't deliver this giant into my hands like he did the stuff in the past. Passion rose up and spoke and David said I don't need your armor or your blessing, all I need is my God.

Some people simply surround you to throw salt on your wounds, shade on your parade and negativity on your dream. Saul thought he was helping, but all he did was add weight to David's destiny. This is the day to get serious, the time to get real. Now is the day to see your destiny fulfilled. This is not just another day; this is your day! Let God be real and every other thing, situation, person or circumstance in your life be a lie. If it does not reflect what God has stated, it is a lie. If you are sick, lie! If you are broke or broken, lie! God said be healed. God said prosper. God said you were able to do anything through Christ who strengthens you! Now is the time to get up and do what God has said do. No more sleep, no more slumber, no more folding of the hands. It's time to get active, get passionate and become more productive.

Daily Declaration

Today will be the best day of my life. Today I declare that I will get more passionate. I will not let people or situations stifle my passion. I will reclaim the passion God gave me. Today will be the best day of my life because I Will Get More Passionate in Jesus' name.

Day 13: **Produce Fruit**
(Matt. 7:15-20)

[15] "Beware of false prophets, who come to you in sheep's clothing, but inwardly they are ravenous wolves.

[16] You will know them by their fruits. Do men gather grapes from thornbushes or figs from thistles?

[17] Even so, every good tree bears good fruit, but a bad tree bears bad fruit.

[18] A good tree cannot bear bad fruit, nor *can* a bad tree bear good fruit.

[19] Every tree that does not bear good fruit is cut down and thrown into the fire.

[20] Therefore by their fruits you will know them.

Day 13: **Produce Fruit**

Passion will cause you to do things you wouldn't normally do like fashion a cord into a whip and clear out the money changers. Passion will drive you to do things like start a business in a bad economy, sell all that you have and put it behind an idea that no one else believes in. Passion will cause you to do crazy things in the eyes of those around you, but you do it because it burns inside if you don't. Passion will make you rise up against the powers that be in church and start ministries that are not traditionally accepted. Passion says go when people say stop and passion says yes when people say no. Now is the time to start following our passion and not people that bear no fruit. Many people will try to tell you what you should do or be doing with your lives, but be careful and watch what they are doing with theirs.

Unproductive people are not the best people to take advice from. Individuals that are in the same place now as they were ten years ago are probably not the best people to direct you. God is about movement, growth and development. We should all be developing constantly in some way. Those that do not develop become cursed or cut down and thrown into the fire. God's Kingdom has no use for unproductive people.

Daily Declaration

Today will be the best day of my life. Today I declare that I will produce fruit. I will not allow anyone to stop me and I will not become stagnate. Today will be the best day of my life because I Will Produce Fruit in Jesus' name.

Day 14: **Produce More Fruit**
(Matthew 21:18-19)

[18] Now in the morning, as He returned to the city, He was hungry.

[19] And seeing a fig tree by the road, He came to it and found nothing on it but leaves, and said to it, "Let no fruit grow on you ever again." Immediately the fig tree withered away.

Day 14: **Produce More Fruit**

Don't be surprised if you move from little to even less. As in the case with the talents Jesus says that, "For to everyone who has, more will be given, and he will have abundance; but from him who does not have, even what he has will be taken away, (Matt. 25:29)." People that bear fruit, normally continue to bear fruit, but unproductive people tend to remain unproductive. Until you allow passion to become your guide and purpose to become your leader there is a good chance that you will simply remain sub-standard, status quo, mediocre, or average.

If you want to excel and bear great fruit and get more than you have ever had and produce more than you ever thought possible, get passionate about what God has put inside you, get passionate about the gifts you have been given, get passionate about the talents you possess and do something with them. Stop waiting for someone else to pull it out of you and trust God to develop you. Be fruitful in and out of season. The fig tree that Jesus cursed wasn't even in season, but Jesus still cursed it for being unproductive. If you are going to be living anyway, you might as well be productive. Get passionate and produce more fruit today!

Daily Declaration

Today will be the best day of my life. Today I declare that I will produce more fruit. I will not give way to the season, instead I will be fruitful in season and out of season. Today will be the best day of my life because I Will Produce More Fruit Jesus' name.

Day 15: **Look with the Prophet's Eyes**
(1 Kings 18:41-45)

[41] And Elijah said to Ahab, "Go, eat and drink, for there is the sound of a heavy rain."

[42] So Ahab went off to eat and drink, but Elijah climbed to the top of Carmel, bent down to the ground and put his face between his knees.

[43] "Go and look toward the sea," he told his servant. And he went up and looked.

"There is nothing there," he said.

Seven times Elijah said, "Go back."

[44] The seventh time the servant reported, "A cloud as small as a man's hand is rising from the sea."

So Elijah said, "Go and tell Ahab, 'Hitch up your chariot and go down before the rain stops you.' "

[45] Meanwhile, the sky grew black with clouds, the wind rose, a heavy rain came on and Ahab rode off to Jezreel.

Day 15: **Look with the Prophet's Eyes**

Elijah looked out over the hills and saw rain. The servant looked out and saw nothing. Elijah possessed the eyes of a prophet, whereas the servant possessed only a natural eye that could only see what was in front of him. The eyes of a prophet see what is possible, whereas the natural eye or the eyes of a servant can only see what is there. It is time for you to make the decision to start looking at life with the eyes of a prophet instead of the eyes of a servant. Instead of seeing what is there, see what is possible.

It doesn't matter if your home is in foreclosure, your spouse left you, your kids don't listen to you and your job is trying to downsize you, you have to start seeing things with the eyes of a prophet. See victory and not distress. See progress and not dismay. You have to see what is not there in order to get some thing you don't have. You might desire to get a better job, start seeing it. You might desire to have a closer walk with Christ, start seeing it. You might desire to get your family in order or your debt destroyed, you might want to start a business or kick a bad habit, whatever it is that you desire you must start seeing it. It all starts in the mind. Once you decide within yourself that you can have something, you can. If you believe that God has spoken something within you and destined you for a great purpose, you need to start believing it and seeing it today. Don't let another day pass you by. Start looking at life with the eyes of the prophet today!

Daily Declaration

Today will be the best day of my life. Today I declare that I will look with the prophet's eyes. I will see what should be there and continue to persevere until it is there. Today will be the best day of my life because I Will Look with the Prophet's Eyes in Jesus' name.

Day 16: **Don't Stop Running**
(1 Kings 18:46)

⁴⁶ The power of the LORD came upon Elijah and, tucking his cloak into his belt, he ran ahead of Ahab all the way to Jezreel.

Day 16: **Don't Stop Running**

In the first part of Acts 1:8, it says that you would receive power once the Holy Spirit came upon you. It is my belief that since you are reading this book, there is a good chance that the Holy Spirit has come upon you and according to the Word of God that means power has also come upon you. Now when the power of God came upon Elijah it gave him the strength and fortitude to run from where he was to where he was going. He ran from Mt. Carmel to Jezreel. It is said that the journey was anywhere from 16-18 miles and took about 2 hours to get there. This means that Elijah ran somewhere around 8.5 miles per hour for 2 hours straight through mud while rain drops were hitting him in the face. If he can do that, I believe you can run through whatever mud your life has created so that you can get to your destination.

Life isn't always easy, but it's possible. Because the power of God has come upon you through the Holy Spirit, you actually possess an unfair advantage in the race. Now is the time and this is definitely the day for you to decide that no matter what life throws your way and no matter what issues hit you in the face, you will not stop running until you reach your destination. You have the power to make it, but you have to decide that you will not stop running. Today is your day.

Daily Declaration

Today will be the best day of my life. Today I declare that I will not stop running. I will continue on my journey no matter what comes my way. Today will be the best day of my life because I Will Not Stop Running in Jesus' name.

Day 17: **Hear the Call**
(John 11:43-44)

[43] Now when He had said these things, He cried with a loud voice, "Lazarus, come forth!"

[44] And he who had died came out bound hand and foot with grave clothes, and his face was wrapped with a cloth. Jesus said to them, "Loose him, and let him go."

Day 17: **Hear the Call**

Lazarus was dead. The mourners had already mourned, the family had buried him, his friends had pronounced him, and they had wrapped him clothes that signified death. He had been placed in a cave with other dead individuals and dead situations. He was surrounded by death and all that came along with it, but the difference between Lazarus and those that were around him is that Lazarus had a call. Lazarus had a word from Jesus. But even though Lazarus had a call, Lazarus still had a decision to make whether or not to hear the call.

As children of God, we have been called to something and given a charge to do something. No matter what people say or what people do, we have a call and the call is all that counts. People can speak against you and try to bury you in insults and negative speech, but the call is all that counts. If I was with you I would preach it like I feel it, but understand that it's all about the call. Don't worry about what they say, don't worry about what they do, you have a call so no matter what happens in life remember that not even the gates of Hell can hold you back because God is in control of everything. Not even death can win against the call. If you have been called, I ask that you listen. Choose to hear the call and obey the call today. Lazarus was not just in a dead situation. He was actually dead, but he heard the call. Perhaps you feel like you are in a dead situation or perhaps you know someone that is, share this word and let them know that even in a dead situation the call can bring life again. Dead situations can live again because of the call of Christ. If you are in a dead situation choose to hear the call and live again.

Daily Declaration

Today will be the best day of my life. Today I declare that I will hear the call. I will not allow my situation to stop me or keep me bound. Today will be the best day of my life because I will Hear The Call in Jesus' name.

Day 18: **Go and Be Great**
(Gen. 8 15-19)

[15] Then God spoke to Noah, saying,

[16] "Go out of the ark, you and your wife, and your sons and your sons' wives with you.

[17] Bring out with you every living thing of all flesh that is with you: birds and cattle and every creeping thing that creeps on the earth, so that they may abound on the earth, and be fruitful and multiply on the earth."

[18] So Noah went out, and his sons and his wife and his sons' wives with him.

[19] Every animal, every creeping thing, every bird, and whatever creeps on the earth, according to their families, went out of the ark.

Day 18: **Go and Be Great**

After the naysayers have spoken, after the rain has fallen and the world has unleashed its worst on you and you still remain standing. Realize that you are standing because God placed you here to triumph. If the rains couldn't drown you and the fire couldn't burn you, if everything you've been through couldn't stop you and all the people that talk about you can't shake you, know that you are here to fulfill the will of God and stand in His greatness.

Now is the time and you are a person that God has called to do great things. It's time to get out of the ark and recover from whatever you've been through. You may have lost some friends during the flood, some cars during the fire, some courage during the battle, but you're still standing. Don't let the past pains or your current fears convince you that what's outside the ark is more than you can handle. God said go! Not only go, but be fruitful and multiply. Do more, produce more and make more than what you had. The old days are dead. Behold a new day. Go and be great. Invest in yourself so that you can develop and become more of a blessing to all those that count on you. Go and be great today!

Daily Declaration

Today will be the best day of my life. Today I declare that I will go and be great. I will not allow my past pains or current fears to hold me back. Today will be the best day of my life because I will Go and Be Great in Jesus' name.

Day 19: **Soar Like the Eagles** (Isaiah 40:28-31)

²⁸ Do you not know? Have you not heard? The Lord is the everlasting God, the Creator of the ends of the earth. He will not grow tired or weary, and his understanding no one can fathom.

²⁹ He gives strength to the weary and increases the power of the weak.

³⁰ Even youths grow tired and weary, and young men stumble and fall;

³¹ but those who hope in the LORD will renew their strength. They will soar on wings like eagles; they will run and not grow weary, they will walk and not be faint.

Day 19: **Soar Like the Eagles**

Oftentimes in life we can allow ourselves to become so weighed down with the concerns of humanity that we forget that we possess a spiritual side that never gets weak or weary. God lives inside of all that hope in Him, meaning those that believe in Him and He strengthens them and encourages them to go on. No matter who you are, whether young or old, man or woman, Jew or Gentile, there comes a time in life where you will get tired. Fatigue can set in your muscles and cause you to longer want to fight the fight or run the race, but God gives strength to those that hope in Him.

Perhaps you have gotten to a place in your life where you stopped hoping or stopped believing in yourself. I encourage you to fight that feeling today and realize that your best days are ahead of you and one of your best days is today because you don't have to be weak. You can allow the Lord to strengthen you by realizing that He has great things in store for you and the negative things are only temporary. Storms might come in life and downturns may take place, but he that hopes in the Lord and trusts Him shall gain renewed strength. Today, if you choose to, you can run and not grow weary, walk and not grow faint. Today, you can soar like the eagles.

Daily Declaration

Today will be the best day of my life. Today I declare that I will soar like the eagles. I will not give into the fatigue of my flesh or the weakness of humanity. Today will be the best day of my life because I will Soar Like The Eagles in Jesus' name.

Day 20: **Display His Splendor**
(Isaiah 61:1-3)

¹ The Spirit of the Sovereign LORD is on me, because the LORD has anointed me to preach good news to the poor. He has sent me to bind up the brokenhearted, to proclaim freedom for the captives and release from darkness for the prisoners,

² to proclaim the year of the LORD's favor and the day of vengeance of our God, to comfort all who mourn,

³ and provide for those who grieve in Zion— to bestow on them a crown of beauty instead of ashes, the oil of gladness instead of mourning, and a garment of praise instead of a spirit of despair. They will be called oaks of righteousness, a planting of the LORD for the display of his splendor.

Day 20: **Display His Splendor**

This passage is prophetically spoken by Isaiah about the coming Messiah, Jesus. He had not yet come, but these are all promises that Jesus was making to his people. He promised that instead of having to wear ashes, He would give his people beauty. Instead of mourning, He would give them gladness and instead of despair, He would give them praise. He promised to do all of these things so that they could display His splendor.

I don't know about you, but I am one of His people. If you are one of His people, choose to display His splendor today. Don't walk around with a sad face or a disappointed countenance. Walk around with your head up and display your crown of beauty. Don't give way to depression or sadness. Smile today because you are anointed with the oil of gladness. Last, but not least, praise God and don't fret, fear or despair. Don't allow life to stress you out today. Choose to display the splendor of God everywhere you go and tell people why. Let them know that Jesus died so that you could live. He was captured so that you could be free and He proclaimed the year of the Lord's favor on you so you could display His splendor. Accept your favor today and display his splendor.

Daily Declaration

Today will be the best day of my life. Today I declare that I will display His splendor. I will not be sad about anything or stress over anything. Today will be the best day of my life because I will Display His Splendor in Jesus' name.

Day 21: **Get Up**
(John 5:2-9)

² Now there is in Jerusalem near the Sheep Gate a pool, which in Aramaic is called Bethesda and which is surrounded by five covered colonnades.

³ Here a great number of disabled people used to lie—the blind, the lame, the paralyzed.

⁴ From time to time an angel of the Lord would come down and stir up the waters. The first one into the pool after each such disturbance would be cured of whatever disease they had.

⁵ One who was there had been an invalid for thirty-eight years.

⁶ When Jesus saw him lying there and learned that he had been in this condition for a long time, he asked him, "Do you want to get well?"

⁷ "Sir," the invalid replied, "I have no one to help me into the pool when the water is stirred. While I am trying to get in, someone else goes down ahead of me."

⁸ Then Jesus said to him, "Get up! Pick up your mat and walk."

⁹ At once the man was cured; he picked up his mat and walked. The day on which this took place was a Sabbath

Day 21: **Get Up**

Jesus presented an opportunity to this man and all he could do was conjure up excuses that explained his situation and excused him for his actions over the course of the last 38 years in which he did nothing but lie there waiting for someone to do what he could have done for himself. Everyday people make excuses of why that can't get where they want to go in life. Motivational speaker Les Brown says, "If you fight for your weaknesses, you get to keep them." Fighting for your weaknesses will get you nothing and making excuses will get you nowhere.

It does not matter if they labeled you mentally retarded as they did Les Brown who makes millions of dollars a year by motivating others. It doesn't matter whether you have been diagnosed with a disease like cyclist Lance Armstrong who had cancer and was given a 40% chance of survival, but beat it and went on to win the Tour De France an astounding 7 times. It doesn't matter what your background is, your race or your physical ailment. The only thing that matters is your desire and your drive. Now is the time to rise up and claim your victory. You don't have to wait for anyone to give you permission to rise and you don't have to bow down to those that despise you for rising. Now is the time to do what God has called you to do. Go with God and be encouraged. Now is the time to get up!

Daily Declaration

Today will be the best day of my life. Today I declare that I will get up. I will not pass up an opportunity do what I have been waiting to do. I will not procrastinate, but I will instead move forward. Today will be the best day of my life because I will Get Up in Jesus' name.

Day 22: **Think Happy Thoughts**
(Philippians 4:4-8)

⁴ Rejoice in the Lord always. Again I will say, rejoice!

⁵ Let your gentleness be known to all men. The Lord is at hand.

⁶ Be anxious for nothing, but in everything by prayer and supplication, with thanksgiving, let your requests be made known to God;

⁷ and the peace of God, which surpasses all understanding, will guard your hearts and minds through Christ Jesus.

⁸ Finally, brethren, whatever things are true, whatever things are noble, whatever things are just, whatever things are pure, whatever things are lovely, whatever things are of good report, if there is any virtue and if there is anything praiseworthy—meditate on these things.

Day 22: **Think Happy Thoughts**

If there is anything praiseworthy, meditate on these things. The word of God is not detached from real life. Jesus endured struggles and hardships and so did His disciples. He knew there would be hard times in life. He even told them that, but in the Word of God as recorded by Paul under the inspiration of the Holy Ghost it says, "if there is anything praiseworthy," meaning if you can find anything in your life to be happy about, "meditate on these things."

The Lord knew that life would be full of struggles, but He was telling us not to focus on them. He says focus on the good stuff. Focus on the things that are noble, lovely and of a good report. Stop focusing on the negative. Focus on the positive. In short, think happy thoughts. Yes, life can bring you down sometimes, but only if you let it. I tell people all the time, "Don't let life keep you from living." Spend today focusing on that quote. Spend today focusing on happy things. Pick out some things in your life that were positive, that were wonderful, and that were awe striking and focus on them. Let's spend today thinking happy thoughts and refusing to let the negatives of this life bring us down. Whatever things are praiseworthy, meditate on these things. Let's just choose to think happy thoughts.

Daily Declaration

Today will be the best day of my life. Today I declare that I will think happy thoughts. I will not allow life to keep me from living. I will overcome negativity with positive thinking. Today will be the best day of my life because I will Think Happy Thoughts in Jesus' name.

Day 23: **Remember What God Has Done (Joshua 4:4-7)**

⁴ So Joshua called together the twelve men he had appointed from the Israelites, one from each tribe, ⁵ and said to them, "Go over before the ark of the LORD your God into the middle of the Jordan. Each of you is to take up a stone on his shoulder, according to the number of the tribes of the Israelites,

⁶ to serve as a sign among you. In the future, when your children ask you, 'What do these stones mean?'

⁷ tell them that the flow of the Jordan was cut off before the ark of the covenant of the LORD. When it crossed the Jordan, the waters of the Jordan were cut off. These stones are to be a memorial to the people of Israel forever."

Day 23: **Remember What God Has Done**

We oftentimes speak of the miraculous parting of the Red Sea when God saved the Israelites from Pharaoh, but we don't speak of the parting of the Jordan as much. God parted the Jordan in order to allow the Israelites to pass over to the land He had promised their forefathers. It was monumental. So monumental in fact that He said gather stones from the middle of the river so that you can always remember this day.

Sometimes in life, in order to get through what is getting ready to come our way, we must remember what God has already done for us. We have to take the time to remember how God parted seas and rivers for us to crossover into where we are now. I'll simplify. We need to remember how God gave us jobs we didn't deserve, made a way when we didn't know how we would get out that situation. We have to remember how God delivered us from things that were too great for us to handle. We have to remember that we have an ally in this battle we call life and that ally has done great things in our past. If we can remember the good days we have had, we can make it to the better days ahead.

David told Saul, "The LORD who delivered me from the paw of the lion and the paw of the bear will deliver me from the hand of this Philistine, (1 Sam. 17:37)." David remembered the great things that God had done for him in the past and he used those memories to propel him forward. Let's focus on what God has done so that we can have the best day today and every day. If He did it once, He can do it again. Remember what God has done for you and allow it to overcome what's in front of you.

Daily Declaration

Today will be the best day of my life. Today I declare that I will remember what God has done. I will not forget how good God has been and how far He has brought me. Today will be the best day of my life because I will Remember What God Has Done in Jesus' name.

Day 24: **Cleanse Your Heart**
(Psalms 51:10-17 and Psalms 103:12)

[10] Create in me a clean heart, O God, and renew a steadfast spirit within me.

[11] Do not cast me away from your presence, and do not take Your Holy Spirit from me.

[12] Restore to me the joy of your salvation, and uphold me by your generous Spirit.

[13] Then I will teach transgressors your ways, and sinners shall be converted to You.

[14] Deliver me from the guilt of bloodshed, O God, The God of my salvation, and my tongue shall sing aloud of Your righteousness.

[15] O Lord, open my lips, And my mouth shall show forth your praise.

[16] For You do not desire sacrifice, or else I would give it; You do not delight in burnt offering.

[17] The sacrifices of God are a broken spirit, A broken and a contrite heart— These, O God, You will not despise.

[12] As far as the east is from the west, so far has He removed our transgressions from us.

Day 24: **Cleanse Your Heart**

This Psalm is a prayer from David to God asking for forgiveness after he had committed adultery with Bathsheba. Who among us has not sinned and felt bad about what we did? On this Christian journey there will be times where we get off track and find ourselves in a place where we are apologizing to God. This is a good step. The problem is that many of us stop there for a while. In my book, *On Track, to the Kingdom* (available at www.Rshamar.com), I deal with this in a little more depth, but for this devotional I will simply say, move on. Ask God for forgiveness and accept it! Don't get knocked off track and stay there. Decide to get over what you did and get on with what you can do. Psalms 103:12 lets us know that when God forgives, He forgives. It is normally us that hold on to the old stuff.

We hold on to past sins, mistakes, short comings and we even hold on to what others did to us or said about us. We have to practice cleansing our hearts daily. Just like most of us take bathes or showers on the daily, we must also allow our hearts to be cleansed daily. Let go of the old stuff so that you can experience the new stuff that God has in store for you. Do not let past occurrences set you back. If it happened yesterday, leave it there. This is a new day, a day that we have never seen before and a day that we will never see again. Let's make the most of this day by cleansing our heart and enjoying this day.

Daily Declaration

Today will be the best day of my life. Today I declare that I will cleanse my heart. I will not allow past pains to hinder me. I will get over my past and allow those things to be washed away. Today will be the best day of my life because I will Cleanse My Heart in Jesus' name.

Day 25: **Forgive**
(Matthew 6:9-15)

[9]"This, then, is how you should pray: " 'Our Father in heaven, hallowed be your name,

[10]your kingdom come, your will be done on earth as it is in heaven.

[11]Give us today our daily bread.

[12]Forgive us our debts, as we also have forgiven our debtors.

[13]And lead us not into temptation, but deliver us from the evil one.'

[14]For if you forgive men when they sin against you, your heavenly Father will also forgive you.

[15]But if you do not forgive men their sins, your Father will not forgive your sins.

Day 25: **Forgive**

Forgiveness is one of the most important facets of Christianity. Our religion is built around the fact that Jesus Christ died on Calvary's cross and shed his blood to cover our sins. His love for us now covers a multitude of sins. Because He loves us, He forgave and forgives us of everything we do. All He asks in return is that we treat others like we want to be treated. The scripture simply states that in order for us to continue to walk in that gift of forgiveness that He gave us, we must also forgive others. In order to enjoy the benefits of Christianity (i.e. peace, grace, love, life) we must forgive.

People walk around every day with unnecessary burdens because they won't forgive people that hurt them. These people have gone on to accept their short comings and have moved on, but for some reason we will continue to walk around holding grudges and hindering ourselves. The Bible says, "let us lay aside every weight," (Heb. 12:1). If we are going to run this race successfully and live a prosperous, productive life, we must lay aside weights. Not forgiving others is a big weight! Don't let other peoples' mistakes hold you back any longer. No matter what they did or how bad they hurt you, let's forgive them today. Don't let another day pass before you forgive those that have done you wrong. Let's practice forgiving on a daily basis.

This is a big one and because of that I want to break the flow of this devotional. Instead of ending this with a daily declaration, let's end it with a prayer:

Father forgive me and help me to forgive others.
I thank you for sending your son to die for me
and because I love Him
and because I thank Him for forgiving me,
I forgive everyone that has hurt me.
I forgive every one that has abused me.
I forgive everyone that has taken advantage of me. I forgive everyone that has ever damaged me in any way.
I love you Lord and I know that you love me
so today I make the declaration
that I will forgive others
as you have forgiven me.
In Jesus' name I pray,
Amen.

Day 26: **Never Give Up**
(Psalms 73:1-3, 13)

¹ Surely God is good to Israel, to those who are pure in heart.

² But as for me, my feet had almost slipped; I had nearly lost my foothold.

³ For I envied the arrogant when I saw the prosperity of the wicked.

¹³ Surely in vain have I kept my heart pure; in vain have I washed my hands in innocence.

Day 26: **Never Give Up**

We see that Asaph was in the midst of a struggle. At one time he had been King David's director of music and Asaph had watched the nation of Israel flourish under David's leadership. He listened to what David said and expected to see God do the great things that David said would come to pass, but instead of seeing the great things that he had been promised he watched as the country was desecrated and to the point of ruin. His brother had been murdered, his people were being enslaved, turmoil was ravaging the nation and Asaph was looking to God wondering what was going on. He started to doubt for just a second the sovereignty of God and started to feel like his faithfulness was all in vain, but if you'll notice in verse 2 he says "almost slipped" and "nearly lost my foothold."

Asaph was a Levite that had seen many things. He had seen both the ups and downs involved with following God, but Asaph still held his footing. He was down, but not out. He was hurting, but he did not give up. As we go through things in life we have to realize that the rain falls on the just as well as the unjust. There will be good days and there will be bad days, but no matter what happens in life we must stand. Do not give up. No matter what comes your way this day, vow not to give up. No matter what you might be dealing with in your life right now, don't give up. There is hope and there is greatness in you. Never give up.

Daily Declaration

Today will be the best day of my life. Today I declare that I will never give up. I will not allow anything to weigh me down to the point that I give up. I will continue to move forward realizing that good things are coming my way. Today will be the best day of my life because I will Never Give Up in Jesus' name.

Day 27: **Focus On the Right Stuff** **(Psalms 73:16-17, 26-28)**

[16]When I tried to understand all this, it was oppressive to me
[17]till I entered the sanctuary of God; then I understood their final destiny.

[26] My flesh and my heart may fail, but God is the strength of my heart and my portion forever. [27]Those who are far from you will perish; you destroy all who are unfaithful to you.
[28]But as for me, it is good to be near God. I have made the Sovereign LORD my refuge; I will tell of all your deeds.

Day 27: **Focus On the Right Stuff**

Forgive the simplicity of the title, but it's imperative that we get it. If we are not focused on the right stuff, we will become consumed with the wrong stuff. It's just that simple. My father told me a long time ago when he was teaching me to drive that whatever I focused on I would drift towards. He said if you focus on the cars and the people walking on the side of the road, you'll drift towards them and perhaps hit them, but if you focus on the road in front of you and where you want to be, that's where you'll go.

Too many times in life we get consumed with what other people have and what other people are doing and we start to drift off course, but God put you here for a reason and he designed a purpose specifically for you and that's all you need to focus on. Focus on what God is speaking in your life and focus on how He's developing you and focus on how you can improve and what areas you lack self-control in. Do not become so concerned with others and the wrong stuff that you begin to feel like less than what you are worth. Asaph was looking at the wicked and seeing how they were prospering and it was bringing his life down because he just didn't understand why God was doing what he was doing, but then he realized something. He realized that God knew what He was doing.

One day this earth will pass away and none of that stuff will matter anymore. We have to do like Asaph did and get our focus back on God. It doesn't matter if you understand what God is doing. All that matters is if you are close to Him. The only thing that matters is if God is your portion and your refuge and all the other stuff will be alright.

Daily Declaration

Today will be the best day of my life. Today I declare that I will focus on the right stuff. I will give into the peace that surpasses all of my understanding and I will allow God to move in my life however He wants to. Today will be the best day of my life because I will Focus On the Right Stuff in Jesus' name.

Day 28: **Inherit What God Promised You (Joshua 1-8)**

¹After the death of Moses the servant of the LORD, the LORD said to Joshua son of Nun, Moses' aide: ²"Moses my servant is dead. Now then, you and all these people, get ready to cross the Jordan River into the land I am about to give to them—to the Israelites. ³I will give you every place where you set your foot, as I promised Moses.

⁴Your territory will extend from the desert to Lebanon, and from the great river, the Euphrates—all the Hittite country—to the Great Sea on the west.

⁵No one will be able to stand up against you all the days of your life. As I was with Moses, so I will be with you; I will never leave you nor forsake you. ⁶"Be strong and courageous, because you will lead these people to inherit the land I swore to their forefathers to give them.

⁷Be strong and very courageous. Be careful to obey all the law my servant Moses gave you; do not turn from it to the right or to the left, that you may be successful wherever you go.

⁸Do not let this Book of the Law depart from your mouth; meditate on it day and night, so that you may be careful to do everything written in it. Then you will be prosperous and successful.

become the Word of God. Your life has to change and the change must start within you. There is a quote that says, "You must become the change you want to see." Inherit the promise of God. You will be prosperous. You will be successful. You will get to where God promised that you would go. Inherit what God promised you and have your best day, today.

Daily Declaration

Today will be the best day of my life. Today I declare that I will inherit what God promised me. I will not look at the past, but I will look at my present and continue to follow God into my future because He has great things in store for me. Today will be the best day of my life because I will Inherit What God Has Promised in Jesus' name.

Day 29: **Hear the Abundance**
(1 Kings 18:41-45)

[41] And Elijah said to Ahab, "Go, eat and drink, for there is the sound of a heavy rain."

[42] So Ahab went off to eat and drink, but Elijah climbed to the top of Carmel, bent down to the ground and put his face between his knees.

[43] "Go and look toward the sea," he told his servant. And he went up and looked.

"There is nothing there," he said.

Seven times Elijah said, "Go back."

[44] The seventh time the servant reported, "A cloud as small as a man's hand is rising from the sea."

So Elijah said, "Go and tell Ahab, 'Hitch up your chariot and go down before the rain stops you.'"

[45] Meanwhile, the sky grew black with clouds, the wind rose, a heavy rain came on and Ahab rode off to Jezreel.

Day 29: **Hear the Abundance**

Perhaps you've tried once and it didn't work. And maybe you went back a second time and it still didn't work. Maybe you even went back a third time, a fourth time, a fifth time and for the very diligent, perhaps you went back a sixth time and still you saw nothing. No change. No results. No improvement. No answer. No reconciliation. No solution. Nothing! But God said, "Go back." He said it through the prophet Elijah then and I believe that He is saying it right now. Go back. Go back to your first love. Return to the God that brought you out before. Trust in Jehovah Rapha, God our healer. Believe in Jehovah Jireh, the Lord our provider. Rely on Jehovah Ezer, the Lord our help.

You may not have seen a change in your health, but God is still a healer. You may not have seen a change in your bank account, but God is still a provider. You might still be wondering how you're going to get out of this situation, but God is a helper. Trust in Him. Go back again, and again, and again, and again, and again, and again until you see something rise up out of the sea. On the seventh time, the servant saw a cloud about the size of a man's hand rise up and from this small cloud a mighty rain came. I am telling you today that I hear the sound of an abundance of rain. Great things are coming your way and you can't give up now or you might not see the rain. Prophet Todd Hall said, "We hear it so that they can see it." I want you to see God move in your life and I know that He will. Continue to seek God and believe for your abundance because I believe that there is an abundance coming your way. Believe it today and live your life in expectancy. May God continue to bless you and keep you forever more.

Daily Declaration

Today will be the best day of my life. Today I declare that I will hear the abundance. I will keep looking until I see the promises of God unfold in my life. Today will be the best day of my life because I will Hear the Abundance in Jesus' name.

Day 30: **Sow a Seed**
(Matthew 3:2-9)

² Such large crowds gathered around him that he got into a boat and sat in it, while all the people stood on the shore.

³ Then he told them many things in parables, saying: "A farmer went out to sow his seed.

⁴ As he was scattering the seed, some fell along the path, and the birds came and ate it up.

⁵ Some fell on rocky places, where it did not have much soil. It sprang up quickly, because the soil was shallow.

⁶ But when the sun came up, the plants were scorched, and they withered because they had no root.

⁷ Other seed fell among thorns, which grew up and choked the plants.

⁸ Still other seed fell on good soil, where it produced a crop—a hundred, sixty or thirty times what was sown.

⁹ He who has ears, let him hear."

Day 30: **Sow a Seed**

Sometimes in life we do things that don't seem to get the expected end that we desired. We plant seed and it gets devoured. We sow, but nothing really develops. But every now and then, we see some things happen because of what we did. Sometimes you might not see the harvest, but you never stop sowing seed. God says that he gives seed to the sower, (2 Cor. 9:10), which means that as long as you continue to do what he has sent you to do He will continue to take care of you. He sent you to sow seed and make disciples of all the nations. God has entrusted us with the task of spreading the Gospel. You can reference scriptures such as Acts 1:8 and Mark 16:15. You must continue to sow seed. Take what you have learned from this devotional and sow it into someone else's life or just give them the devotional.

As followers of God we must be sure to continue to be a blessing to others and give as God has blessed us to give. Sow a seed into someone's life today. Be a blessing to someone. You never know what people are dealing with and you never know how one gesture can change someone's life.

I heard a preacher describe a seed as a piece of our present that we sow in order to receive a greater return in our future. Sow a seed today so that you will have something to look forward to in the future. God bless you.

Daily Declaration

Today will be the best day of my life. Today I declare that I will sow a seed. I will let go of what I have and send it out so that it can have a greater effect and return in a greater way. Today will be the best day of my life because I will Sow a Seed in Jesus' name.

Keep Going
Your Best Days Are Now

We thank you for choosing this ministry. Remember, it is your help and donations that make it possible for us to function so please continue to sow into this ministry through your tithes, offerings and financial gifts. Contact us at:

Better Way Ministries
PO Box 223
Lovejoy, GA 30250
678-559-9193

AuthorRonWalker@gmail.com
www.AuthorRonWalker.com
@AuthorRonWalker

Thank you and God Bless you,

Rev. Ron Walker
Pastor

"There is a Better Way to Live, Love and Do Business"

Printed in Great Britain
by Amazon

Day 28: **Inherit What God Promised You**

Many of you reading this devotional have had things promised to you and prophesied over your life, but you have yet to see them come to pass. You have watched as others moved into their destiny and you have witnessed individuals move into their purpose, but your life is still mundane and rudimentary, but you are believing God for some great things to come your way. I want you to start inheriting the promise today. Start embracing your change. Start accepting your deliverance and your prosperity because it is still coming your way. When Moses died, it set Joshua up for an inheritance.

There are some things in your life that will have to die in order for you to receive the inheritance that God has for you. "Be strong and courageous," (v6), the Lord told Joshua because there is a responsibility associated with the inheritance. People will be watching. Not everyone is ready for the responsibility, but if you are, pay attention to verse 8. You must study the Word of God, embody the Word of God and